ON THE ROLE OF SPIRITUALITY IN PURSUING A PERSONALLY SATISFYING LIFESTYLE

BY

LEWIS E. AALDERS, DOCTOR OF PHILOSOPHY
THE HELP & PLEASE LEARNING CENTRE
KENTVILLE, NOVA SCOTIA, CANADA

LEWIS@AALDERS.CA

RoseDog Books
PITTSBURGH, PENNSYLVANIA 15222

ISBN # 0-8059-9344-4
Printed in the United States of America

First Printing

For information or to order additional books, please write:
RoseDog Books
701 Smithfield St.
Pittsburgh, PA 15222
U.S.A.
1-800-834-1803
Or visit our web site and
on-line bookstore at www.rosedogbookstore.com

DEDICATION

This Booklet is humbly dedicated to the very many various females from whom, collectively, I have learned the practical essence of a human life. These include especially the following:

1) Catherine A. O. Hebb, to whom I was married in 1954, and from whom I was divorced in 1968;

2) Teresa Zuchniewicz, to whom I was married in 1976, and from whom I was divorced in 1977;

3) M. Violeta Caamano, with whom I lived common-law from 1982 until 1991;

4) Vivian M. Pike, with whom I lived common-law from 1991 until 2001;

5) and finally to my dear Mother, the former Bernice D. (Huntley) Aalders, who died in 1992 at the age of 84 years.

May all of these women rest in Peace and Tranquility,
for ever more!

Lewis E. Aalders, Ph. D.
Kentville, Nova Scotia, Canada

Table of Contents

Religion and Science

Religious truth and scientific theory often seem to be incompatible.
If one of them is basically incorrect, then why do we support both
so vigorously?

Religious "truths" and/or instructions are supposedly passed on
from GOD to those human recipients who are attuned to receiving
them. Such truths are then passed on to other humans as "God's
Word". It is claimed that these instructions and/or truths are not
subject to change through the ages. They are supposed to hold for
all time.

Scientific information originates quite differently. It is based on
human interpretation of human observations and designed experiments. Such theories are always subject to review, and modifica-
tions and/or alternate explanations are routinely entertained.

The two methods of gaining information upon which one can
guide one's life are, in my mind, extremely difficult to reconcile, if in
fact they are not mutually exclusive. The focal point, in my opinion,
concerns the origin of life, particularly of human life. It is hard to
believe that life was initiated by special creation in a period of six days,
on the one hand, and also that it originated spontaneously and developed over millions of years through genetic evolution, on the other.

It seems to me that, if one of these explanations is accurate, or
close to being accurate, then the alternate explanation is wildly
incorrect. One is based on human observations, which readily
invites further relevant observation and experiment, whereas the
other is based on what God told somebody in a supposedly private
communication. Both explanations are highly susceptible to variation in human interpretation of the data. But one invites corrective
modification by anyone willing to undertake the job, whereas the
other is considered unchangeable, to be "written in stone".

1

If one or the other of these explanations is patently wrong, then why in the world does our society entertain and/or support both of them so vigorously? Do we have to resort, like Prometheus, upon "false hopes" in an effort to prop up our struggling civilization? Do we end up having to "live a lie?"

Orders, Requests, and Suggestions: Your response depends on how you ask

If a person cannot, or does not, want to cooperate with someone else's attempt to move them to action, they might try to (1) ignore the attempt if it seems to be a Suggestion, (2) negotiate an acceptable alternative if it seems to be a Request, or (3) follow their own good common sense if it seems to be an unacceptable Order.

When someone attempts to cause you to take some specific action, the attempt can typically be classified rather easily as either an Order, a Request, or a Suggestion. Whether your reaction will please them or not will depend in part on how their wishes are presented initially.

We all recognize what **ORDERS** are. "Suzie, go clean your room!", "Whoa!", and "Be quiet!" are all examples. Orders, when written, are usually followed by an exclamation mark(!). When that mark is missing, you can safely consider that it is at least understood.

A **REQUEST** is a softer attempt to cause you to take a specific action. I consider the word "please" to be a part of the wording of every request, be it written, spoken, or at least understood. "Please be seated", "Johnny, please close the door", and "please drive more carefully" are all examples of typical requests.

SUGGESTIONS tend to be more variable in character. Whereas Orders are assigned grammatically to "the Imperative mode", Suggestions are assigned grammatically to "the Subjunctive mode". That is, Suggestions are typically associated with the words "if" and "would", as in "If so-and-so, then would you like...". "Would you like a cup of tea?", "Would you be willing to serve as a witness? " or "Maybe this brush would work better than that knife", would all be classified as suggestions. Again, very often the word "if" is understood but not spoken or written, and that is also sometimes the case with the word "would".

The tone of voice is another major factor in determining whether an attempt to cause action should be considered a Suggestion, a Request or an Order. If someone said to you gently and in a quiet questioning voice "Eat your peas?", then you might interpret that as meaning "would you be willing to eat your nice peas, if I wanted you to?". With a slightly firmer voice, but with exactly the same wording, you might interpret the message as a Request, a plea: "Please eat your peas". But if delivered in a very firm voice, the exact same words "Eat your peas" could mean : "Eat your #!%$! peas, if you know what's good for you". Further interpretation of the character of the other person's message may be gained by an assessment of the expression on their face. A teasing smile might indicate love, whereas a severe frown would be expected to indicate anger and/or fear. So the words used, the tone of voice, and the facial expression, all help us interpret the character of the incoming message, and whether we should classify it as an Order, a Request or a Suggestion.

Upon receiving a Suggestion or a Request or an Order, it is appropriate, if the action wished for is acceptable to yourself, to agree and to act in accordance with the other person's wishes. The real rub comes, however, when you are not at all inclined to do as they want. I would not want to be so presumptuous as to give you firm rules to follow in cases like that, but some ideas are surely worth consideration.

A SUGGESTION can often merely be shrugged off, as in "Huh?", or "Oh, I don't think so", or "I'm too busy right now". That type of answer will often take care of their attempt in a reasonably satisfactory way. However, if the other person then utters the one magic word, "Please", then the Suggestion will have been upgraded immediately to a Request, and it should then be dealt with as such.

With a sincere REQUEST, I prefer personally never to reply with a simple unmodified "no", or to simply ignore the request. Depending on circumstances, that would seem to me often to be considered a rather direct insult. Rather, if I really didn't want to cooperate with the Request, I would try to start negotiating an alternate course of action that would hopefully be acceptable to both of us. Sometimes this works out quite satisfactorily, and sometimes it does not. If it does work out, then that is just fine. If it doesn't, well, it may be more acceptable to end up failing after honest negotiations than to have merely dismissed the request with a cold "no". Occasionally, the other person will be determined enough after failed negotiations to upgrade their request to the level of an Order. And then things get more serious.

By its very nature, a serious ORDER is something that is really non-negotiable. You might attempt to downgrade their message to a Request by smiling back mockingly, or by making some smart aleck remark, but the other person might not take too kindly to that. You mostly have one of two choices: either (1) you can swallow your pride and do as you have been told, in spite of the fact that you don't want to, or (2) you can refuse to carry out the Orders that have been assigned to you, and then prepare immediately to handle whatever consequences may or may not follow.

Hopefully, the other person might then back down. On the other hand, they might try to force you into action by physical effort, or by threat, or whatever. And then very quickly, you should take into consideration whatever conditions might ensue: getting beat up and suffering physical injury, the pride of having stood up successfully for your own rights, the praise or condemnation of your friends and family and society, the pain of possible guilt and/or shame, and any other considerations that might seem to be of importance to you. Basically, you will decide either to fight or to flight. That will be a very personal decision, and you may have to live with the results for a long, long time. Usually, if you choose not to do as you have been directed, it is wise to try to just walk away. And at other times it may be wise to go on the offensive. And there are occasions about which, when the smoke clears, you soothe your anger by telling the world of your frustrations. You might try to organize some kind of major public protest.

If a person cannot, or does not, want to cooperate with someone else's attempt to move them to action, they might try to (1) ignore the attempt if it seems to be a Suggestion, (2) negotiate an acceptable alternative if is seems to be a Request, or (3) follow their own good common sense if it seems to be an unacceptable Order. And the wiser you are, and the luckier you are, the better your chances for a satisfactory outcome. But when the chips are down, and all is considered, there are things in life whose protection, I believe, are well worth a very determined fight.

Adolescent Sex Education

Traditional attempts at sex education have proven ineffective in reducing incidents of teenage pregnancy and venereal disease. An alternate mode of sex education, known as "outercourse", may prove more effective in achieving these desired goals.

The traditional method of sex education that has been used most widely in North American schools is based essentially on two principles. The first principle is "Don't!", and the second principle is "but if you do, these are some of the really awful diseases that you are likely to catch!". And it seems that rather extreme scare tactics are commonly used in describing such diseases. Further, the "very fragile nature" of condoms is then demonstrated by rolling condoms down over the rather sharp protrusions at the tip of a banana. If some condoms get punctured in the process, well, that just emphasizes that you should never trust condoms! And that seems to be about all that most traditional sex education courses consist of.

On the surface of it all, that sounds quite okay. Kids are told what to do and what not to do. What more can you say? But the essential point here is that in study after study after study, when the results of such courses are actually measured against a standard, the pregnancy and disease incidence following such traditional courses has been found to be no different than where no sex education of any kind had been offered. In other words, the "don't do it!" courses may make the teachers feel real good, but they have no measurable effect whatsoever on the students.

The term "outercourse" has been around for a few years. It is similar in meaning to sexual intercourse, with the one major exception that the male partner's penis and the female partner's vagina are never allowed to touch each other. Everything else is fully acceptable, including kissing, necking, petting, manual masturbation, and oral sex (both cunnilingus and blow jobs).

When adolescents reach the age of puberty, the changes that take place gradually within their bodies are really huge. You can readily see the physical changes, but the hidden emotional changes are just as dramatic. In evolutionary history, that is the age at which sexuality and reproduction began. And today, our urge to initiate heterosexual intercourse at that age is just as strong as it was for adolescents many thousands of years ago. But our society today consistently says "No! Wait for ten years! And then you can get married. And only then will we approve of you having sex."

That situation gets really frustrating for young teenagers. Why cannot they have sex? Especially if they promise to be very careful about it? And many unhappy teenagers, or even most, will try experimenting with sex on the sly, and with little or no knowledge of the standard caveats that should be followed. Traditionally, society has conspired against young people by keeping all knowledge of sex and birth control completely out of their reach. And kids having sex with little or no knowledge of the subject can readily be predicted to get into real trouble.

Church teachings have traditionally been the most effective curbs on teenage sexuality. But with the development of the birth control pill in the 1950s, and with the steady decline in church attendance in recent years, the church is having less and less influence on teenage sexuality. But the hormonally driven frustrations are still there in strength, and with the religious curbs against them being less and less effective, such frustrations are expressed more and more as teenage rebellion, violence, vandalism, and the ever increasing use of alcohol and other mood influencing drugs. The situation is not at all a pretty one, and it has the vibrant potential to get a whole lot worse.

With outercourse activity, there are two separate phases. There is "the giving phase" and there is "the receiving phase". In the giving phase, the boy may initiate activity by touch or by word of mouth. The girl should feel perfectly free, either (1) to allow the boy to continue, (2) to not allow the boy to continue, or (3) to suggest conditions under which he may continue. Having been the initiator and with permission to proceed, he then has the obligation to provide for her the most acceptable outercourse experience that he possibly can. If at any time during such activities the girl begins to suspect that he is pleasuring himself at her expense, then she should feel free to ask him to cease, to stop, to quit. And of course he is obligated to do just that. If he refuses or protests at all, then she should consider dropping that guy and finding herself a new outercourse partner.

Similarly, when the girl wishes to pleasure the boy, she should devote herself completely to providing the very best possible experience for him. Once her finger makes physical contact with his penis, she should strive to continue pleasuring him until he reaches a satisfactory orgasm.

After a boy and girl have known each other favorably and for quite a reasonable length of time, and a comfortable level of honesty, trust and respect has been established between them, they will probably want to experiment with full sexual intercourse. With proper use of a condom, this should be reasonably safe physically, but there may be a different mental dynamic. The girl should realize that, once his penis has entered her vagina, her partner may behave somewhat like an arrow released from the nock of a bow. It is going to speed rapidly and directly to the target, and it would require a major effort to alter it from that course. After such an experience, the girl may have the uncomfortable feeling that she has been "used", simply as a means to satisfy a male's lust. Other males (hopefully) might exercise better self control and be much more responsive to the girl's feelings and wishes.

With adequate birth control, a well matched couple might choose ultimately to dispense with condoms altogether and to enjoy full scale sexual activities unencumbered. This happy situation might continue for some extended period of time provided that both partners are fully open and honest with each other, and that they maintain a very high level of mutual trust and respect.

It would be of great help to teenagers who are really trying to do the responsible thing if their parents would "come on board". Parents might help by (1) giving their child moral permission to carry on outercourse activities, as appropriate. (2) offering to help the inexperienced child and the child's partner to learn whatever is necessary to carry on such activities safely. (3) offering to help screen potential outercourse partners before any physical activity is begun. (4) offering to protect the couple from interruptions and/or intrusions during their intimate activities. (5) offering to monitor certain outercourse activities to guard against the possibility of force or coercion being used. And especially (6) being open to non-judgmental discussion of anything and everything that the child would like to discuss.

On the Question of Anger, Violence, and Addictive Behavior:
A common subversion of the normal, healthy, reproductive instinct

Evolution by natural selection has developed in all of us a very strong instinctive drive to seek, find, and develop an intimate and trusting relationship with a person of the opposite gender. When this drive is thwarted, anger, violence, and/or addictive behavior are the usual results. Improved attitudes toward the raising of children are urgently needed, and some helpful suggestions are presented.

The compulsion to take drugs beyond medical advice in order to produce desired effects, or to prevent the onset of ill effects that occur when they are not taken, is the usual basis of drug abuse. Such use can well lead on to full blown drug addiction.

The changes that take place in a person's body during and shortly after the period of adolescence make that person especially susceptible to addictive behavior. To understand addictive behavior, we can look back to our evolutionary past. Not just to the past thousand years or so, but back maybe 50 to 100 thousand years. Evolution is normally an extremely slow process, and our basic instinctive behaviors were essentially developed way back in those ancient times. Evolutionary developments during the past thousand years might well be considered then as merely a "fine tuning" of our genetically controlled impulses.

Within a person's body at about the time of puberty, a series of hormonal changes "kicks in", as specific genes are automatically "turned on", producing a very strong continuing impulsive drive to seek out and establish a close intimate relationship with at least one accepting person of the opposite sex. Without such a relationship, we tend then to wander, looking for we know not what, but continuing to explore on with a high level of curiosity and determination. Hopefully, some day we find what we have been looking for, - a person with whom we can and do develop a very loving and trusting intimate relationship. And following the establishment of that relationship, offspring are likely to be produced. And the genetic complement that gave rise to our strong drive to wander, seek, and find an accepting partner, will be passed on to the next generation, thus continuing the human life cycle.

But now, if that drive to wander, seek, find, and establish a rewarding relationship with a person of the opposite sex were somewhat weak, then the genes driving that weaker type of behavior would be passed on to the next generation at a much lower frequency than those of the person who was striving on with more determination. That is because they would on average produce fewer children. And gradually, over many generations, the genes pushing the urge to strive on with strong determination would outnumber those for low determination, and that type of change in gene frequency over time is precisely what we mean by the expression "evolution by natural selection".

At about the time of puberty, the adolescent is likely to receive in school what is popularly known as "sex education". Now, there may be, here and there, some very adequate programs of sex education given in schools, but I have never personally heard of one. Typically, when the sex education programs that are given in schools have been evaluated for their effectiveness in controlling pregnancy and child birth, they are shown to have had no overall effect whatsoever on the subsequent behavior of the students. The parents and teachers may consider them to be wonderful, but to the students, they are usually considered useless, or sometimes even laughable. Ideally, it is usually considered that parents should fill the role of sex educator. In practice, however, that ideal situation is rarely fulfilled. In many cases, maybe even in most cases, the parents would dearly love to fulfill that role in a most adequate way, but the knowledge and skill necessary to do so is just not there.

More typically, the adolescent is led off to the church of the parents' choice, which they probably haven't frequented in years, and the adolescent is introduced to "the required teachings". He or she then gets coerced into "getting right with the Lord" by being baptized, or confirmed, or whatever. The parents then feel that they have done their job adequately, or at least as adequately as they were capable of doing it. A great many adolescents are put through this same standard ritual, probably mostly because it is a long cherished tradition in many families.

That futile gesture is only the initial stage of the religious coercion that is typically fostered upon all young couples who wish to get involved in intimate relations. With all of the fervor that they can muster, religiously oriented but well meaning people continually push the biblical principle of "no sex outside of marriage". And the young people, wanting desperately to partake of sex, but not wanting to court societal disapproval, will often agree to come to church, and for that one reason only, will "tie the required religious and legal knot". With a high expectation for improved opportunities for more and better sex, and all of that with full societal approval, they vow to love each other for ever and ever, "till death do us part". The motivation for marriage having been mostly the hope for more and better sex, each hungry partner has a very strong tendency to push for his or her own greatest personal satisfaction, even if it is at the expense of the other. Usually, little consideration is given to the thought that if they concentrate on pleasing their partner, then their partner will, in turn, concentrate on pleasing them. Even though that is the required basis for a long and happy marriage, the trust that is necessary for that principle to kick into action is rarely present. Punctuating that conclusion is the fact that more than half of all marriages break down and are followed by divorce. When "the honeymoon is over", the couple is not nearly so trusting of the undying love of each other as they were before the honeymoon began. And the trust, once broken, is very difficult to regain.

After a few incidents of trust extended, and then trust broken, it becomes more and more difficult for either partner to develop trust in anyone of the opposite sex. In a world where evolution by natural selection is driving them constantly to seek and find a suitable partner with whom to establish a mutual trusting and intimate relationship, they become suspicious and wary of even a very promising prospective partner. The extreme frustration of such a situation becomes a strong incentive for them to try to soothe their painful feelings with alcohol, tobacco, cocaine, or whatever else is offered.

The instinctive drive toward a normal healthy reproduction of the human species thus often gets subverted into a physically damaging addiction to chemical substances. And all of this mostly brought about, let me suggest, by misdirected religious influence.

Attempts to preach the good line to students in the schools with respect to drug abuse has been tried very extensively in some areas, but a clear measure of its effectiveness is very difficult to evaluate. In some cases, it may produce some beneficial effects, but in others, it is claimed to have done more harm than good. What students really want is some reasonable understanding of what is going on within their bodies, and permission to handle those feelings in ways that the student is free to choose for himself or herself. And of course it goes without saying that that permission is exactly what the parent is not willing to give. The protective impulses of the parents kick in strongly, and they entertain such thoughts as, "That would be far too dangerous! They don't have the necessary knowledge to handle loaded situations like that". And as things go today, you would have to have some sympathy for that parental point of view.

But supposing that children, from the age of beginning to walk, were given honest answers to all questions that they might ask about aspects of sexuality and reproduction. None of this "The baby was brought to us by a stork!", or "You can learn all that when you get older", or "Little girls should be seen but not heard", and so on, and so on. If bringing up a child were considered more a process of helping them to learn in an accurate way how the world operates, and less a matter of indoctrinating them to behave in the way that we were urged to behave when we were small (but never did), then perhaps there would be less anger, addiction, and violence in the world.

Some educators have emphasized the principle of encouraging children to learn to make their own decisions from a very early age. Early decisions should be very simple ones, such as whether to wear the blue sweater or the green one. As the child gets used to making decisions, they can be allowed to make more and more of them, and more and more significant ones. And with practice comes skill. By the time the child reaches adolescence, he or she could not only be making quite good decisions, but if left consistently to carry out the decisions made, would be rather skilled at deciding whether to accept or reject advice given by parents and by others. If parental advice offered over the years had proven to be very helpful, the child would have learned to seek and consider parental advice very carefully. But if it had proven to be of little help, then could you blame the young person for going elsewhere to seek his or her desired advice?

In any case, the resulting outcome, I believe, should be adults much better educated, and with much better judgment, than most of those being turned out in the world today. And maybe more people would honor their healthy drive toward sexual activity, and not subvert it into an addiction to physically damaging chemical drugs and the accompanying frustration, anger, sickness, and violence that tends to go with all of that.

The Second Coming of the Lord:
We have been waiting a long time

Personal salvation is based on belief alone, and the process of attaching behavioral requirements to belief for purposes of salvation is considered to be a corruption of the message of Jesus. Principles of acceptable behavior evolve, and should be established democratically.

Religious belief and practice have been the strategy by which mankind has survived over the ages. To choose the time to plant, the strategy for harvesting game, or how to handle a physical challenge, it is wise to consider how others have chosen in the past, and how the results of that choice have turned out. Some "others" have been more successful than other "others", and we tend to repeat and imitate the behaviors of the "wise" ones, and to avoid those of the lesser ones. In time, the "wisdom of the wise" has become rather deeply ingrained in our society.

Wise leaders attract followers, and followers tend to follow the advice of wise leaders, without necessarily understanding the "why" of their advice. Behavior thus tends to be fixed by authority, and not always by reason. Until conditions change significantly, that tends to be a highly successful strategy. Communities prosper and grow!

But over time, conditions DO tend to change. Successful strategies become less and less successful. Some creative persons will modify accepted behavior in an attempt to improve their degree of success. Others will stick to the old ways. And a process of "survival of the fittest" will tend to follow, similar to what occurs following a genetic mutation. Most genetic mutations are harmful, and are eventually eliminated from the population. Cultural mutations may or may not be detrimental, and at times may be adopted very quickly and completely throughout a community.

Tens of thousands of differing religious traditions have been identified throughout the history of mankind. Such traditions have been based essentially on behavior, and a personal conformity to accepted behavior or a deviation from it. In modern days, we speak of, and value very highly, the principle of "personal freedom". The opposing principle of force, or punishment, or fear of such, has been used throughout the ages to direct or motivate specific behavior from others. When behavior approved by society (i.e. virtuous behavior) is taught to growing children deliberately and with vigor, a strong sense of "conscience" is built up within the child's mind. If later expressed behavior deviates significantly from those absorbed virtuous principles, uncomfortable feelings of guilt and/or shame tend to develop, and are often associated with fear of possible societal punishment.

They say that "misery likes company". A person alone with guilt, shame, and/or fear can suffer great discomfort, even a disabling discomfort. If and when such afflicted persons share their difficulties with others, they open themselves up with great vulnerability to the judgment of those others. The tendency is to not share one's difficulties with any person for fear of condemnation, and the discomfort thus tends to build. If on the other hand, they should share their difficulties with a compassionate and loving person, some forgiveness is hopefully obtained, and the discomfort tends to subside. But where to find such a compassionate, understanding, and loving person?

Jesus of Nazareth was such a person, and I am led to believe that other leaders have been also, though to a lesser degree. "Miracles" were a conspicuous method by which Jesus convinced others of his great powers of healing. His willingness to die for his beliefs, even in the face of great physical punishment, convinced others that he was truly the "Son of God", and that he died willingly to atone for the sins of mankind.

Unfortunately, much of the descriptions concerning Jesus and his teachings, I believe, have been symbolic and metaphorical in nature, and require considerable interpretation. My understanding of his message is that personal belief in him and his ways is the cornerstone to his healing power, and that true behavioral adherence by a believer to that believer's own personal conscience as tempered by meditation is the source of great power, - of the type that Jesus demonstrated so convincingly.

His later followers, however, have tended to emphasize the importance of good deeds in addition to belief as being of supreme importance. My sense is that good deeds tend to follow a firm belief in Jesus' teachings, but are not an essential ingredient for personal salvation. Over the years, unfortunately, his followers have tended strongly to add behavioral requirements to the recipe for healing in a self-serving attempt to control the behavior of their respective followers.

The downfall of all of this is that wise behavior, in order to maintain its wisdom, needs to be modified from time to time to reflect changing conditions. And behavioral requirements "written in stone" just do not change at all. The coming of the Industrial Revolution, and the introduction of modern technology have certainly introduced significant changes into our conditions for living. By tying ancient behavioral messages to teachings concerning beliefs, modern theologians have thus tended to corrupt the teachings of Jesus to such a degree that they are largely unacceptable to much of today's modern citizenry.

With much improved education, experience, and meditation, I believe most persons could become wise enough to be considered as "gods" in their own right. Other persons might choose to follow the god of their choice, be it Jesus or other. With freely chosen learning without indoctrination, such "gods" could well decide for themselves what is "right" and what is "wrong". And if they were to communicate honestly, openly, and freely with each other, and reason together with mutual respect, and without resorting to threats of force or punishment, it should be possible to establish acceptable community standards of right and wrong in a democratic way, and to modify those standards from time to time as suggested by reason.

New ideas and suggestions concerning behavior would be expected to arise from time to time, should be discussed and evaluated, and accepted standards be allowed to evolve in a process of "survival of the most reasonable". And by what better principle could behavioral requirements be established and maintained for the long-term survival of a sustainable civilization??

The Gospel, According to Lew:
A modern examination of an old text

The Biblical description of the activities and life of Jesus have been read too literally by many of today's theological scholars. Some reasonable interpretation adds needed credibility to most of those faith inspiring stories.

In the Christian Bible, we read (KJV, John 14), "Jesus saith unto him, 'I am the way, the truth, and the life; no man cometh unto the Father, but by me. If ye had known me, ye should have known my Father also: and from henceforth ye know him, and have seen him.'"

And do you remember Mohandas K. Gandhi, the great spiritual leader of India? To a comment that implied that he, as a Hindu, was a better Christian than are most professed Christians, Gandhi is reported to have replied, "I am a Christian and a Hindu and a Moslem and a Jew". Obviously, Gandhi considered these four supposedly distinct religions all to be teaching essentially the same message.

In claiming that "I am the way, the truth, and the life", I believe that Jesus meant to convey the idea that his attitude toward life was the correct one: it was accurately based on truth: and thus his way of living was the appropriate way to go. And by saying, "No man cometh unto the Father, but by me", I believe that he was trying to say that nobody gets to experience a really heavenly way of living, unless he actually lives according to the same pattern of spiritual love that Jesus was demonstrating."

Jesus further explained that, "In my Father's house are many mansions: if it were not so, I would have told you. I go to prepare a place for you. And if I go and prepare a place for you, I will come again, and receive you unto myself; that where I am, there ye may be also."

In the Book of Revelations, as we all know, a detailed description is presented of a whole series of supernatural events that are predicted to be associated with the future earthly return of Jesus. But in contrast to traditional belief in those days, most well trained scientists of today have great difficulty believing seriously in supernatural miracles. We realize more and more now that there seems to be solid cause and effect for every recognized happening.

As Albert Schweitzer expressed it clearly before I was born, "We are obliged to admit the evident fact that religious truth varies from age to age". "We of today do not, like those who were able to hear the preaching of Jesus, expect to see a Kingdom of God realizing itself in supernatural events. Our conviction is that it can only come into existence by the power of the spirit of Jesus working in our hearts and in the world". "It is the destiny of Christianity to develop through a constant process of spiritualization".

Most scientists can well remember since a very early age, having been told as truthful many stories involving supernatural events. Everything that they have learned since then has had to be filtered through those early teachings. Accordingly, some have a challenging time currently in surrendering the idea of an external living God governing our personal lives on a daily basis. While the logic of science can never, by nature, prove the non-existence of such an external living God, neither to my knowledge has any hard evident ever been offered to support the existence of such an external force.

Except for those with specialized knowledge of the field, few persons appreciate the great power of natural selection over the long term to originate, mold, shape, and fine tune such very specialized organs as the animal eye and the human brain. Without such appreciation, the idea of an external supernatural "designer" seems to them almost necessary as the only possible explanation for that greatest of all eternal mysteries.

As for the principle of supernatural spirits living on forever, after we have become physically deceased and all memory and record of our individual behaviors and life experiences have been extinguished, I would consider that our personal spirits have become dead and gone. It is only if our recorded life behavior and accomplishments have been sufficiently remarkable and distinct so as to be perpetuated into posterity that our spirit may, as promised, "live on forever". The spirit of Jesus will undoubtedly live forever, and ours might also if we choose and actually do live a life dedicated to the kind of spiritual love that Jesus demonstrated for us. There is real power in that sort of life, and that power grows with unexpected strength as we try with diligence continually to expand our spiritual love for others, and through understanding to conquer the fear that seems always to be associated with our normal daily living. Additionally, such a way of life provides fertile ground for the development of what is generally known as "personal wisdom".

A hundred years ago, we had little or no understanding as to the mechanism by which various traits got inherited from generation to generation. But by now, we have developed a much more complete understanding of how that all works. Similarly, we at present do not understand at all clearly how the human brain accomplishes the tasks that it seems to accomplish so very easily. At this point, that all remains as a great mystery. But with continued study and experimentation, we may hopefully one day develop a good biochemical understanding of how the human brain works to accomplish all of those marvelous things. Thus, the future of our evolutionary development and understanding would seem to offer a possible potential to become magnificent beyond our wildest dreams. But then, that future may be possible only if and when more and more of us practice a kind of love of the type that was so convincingly demonstrated by the remarkable life of Jesus.

On Aspects of Prostitution, Bigamy, and Covenant Relationships: It seems that we all would prefer a more adequate sex life

The mental component of the male sexual drive is not well satisfied within a prostitution format of sexual activity. Other types of heterosexual relationships are examined herein, and their supposed strengths and weaknesses outlined. A "covenant" type of relationship would seem to be the most comfortable and long lasting type of marital relationship.

Factors related to sexuality are recognized as major factors in determining the direction of human evolutionary change. It is through sexual activity and the subsequent successful rearing of resulting progeny that genetic factors are either maintained or changed gradually over succeeding generations. Through natural selection, genetic factors promoting increased long term reproductive success are rewarded, and genetic factors reducing that success are similarly reduced.

In some animal groups, the mink family for example, sexual activity is carried on by what we might recognize as "forced rape". Females in heat are routinely raped and made pregnant by aggressive males. Males of all species seem to compete vigorously for the privilege of engaging in such activity, and the most aggressive males are the ones that get their aggression-causing genes passed on to the next generation in highest numbers. With human males, this urge to forcible rape females is moderated by a consideration of later guilt and by the threat of severe physical punishment inflicted generously by a horrified society.

Nevertheless, with some few males, especially if taunted by other males or even females, and possibly under the influence of alcohol or other drugs, the urge to rape a female becomes overwhelming, even in the face of possible punishment. And so it happens now and then, and most people, shocked to the core, just cannot understand how any man could inflict such "cruel and inhuman treatment" on any other person.

In primate species, the control of sexual activity is considered to be centered primarily in the so-called "reptilian part" of the brain. Within human brains, additional anatomical components have evolved over time which control other aspects of brain activity, but sexuality seems still to be controlled largely by that ancient brain component. Our basic sexual drives are accordingly surprisingly similar to those of earlier evolved types, and it is significant to note that, on a sexual level, we still respond very much faster and more completely to "body language" than we do to the spoken word.

In most mammalian species, strong dominance hierarchies are usually in evidence. With wolves, for example, only one male (the alpha male) and only one female (the alpha female) in each family pack get to breed successfully. The alpha male and the alpha female wolves are normally of about the same size, and they have a monogamous relationship. With elephant seals, on the other hand, the dominant male is very much larger than any female, and he maintains a large harem of breeding females. In considering many other species, there is somewhat of a graduated series where the number of females breeding with one male seems to be associated rather closely with the specific difference in size between the dominant male and the average breeding female. Human males on average are somewhat larger than average females, and on that rough animal scale, one might expect one dominant human male to breed with precisely two breeding females. And how does that insight translate to human activity as we see it in every day operation?

The cultural norm in our western world is a monogamous relationship, that is, one male per one female. But in evaluating various other human cultures throughout the world, it has been claimed that more than half of them allow a male to have a second legal wife. That is, if he wishes to do so and can arrange it, he is free to maintain a bigamous relationship with two wives concurrently.

Within the human male psyche, let me suggest that sexual satisfaction is composed of both a physical component and a mental component. The physical component is hormonally driven, is usually strongest in the teen years, and is expected to decrease in strength gradually thereafter as production levels of testosterone drop off. This element of sexual drive is satisfied by experiencing occasional sexual orgasms, regardless of how they may be achieved. Masturbation and/or "wet dreams" seem to work adequately for this purpose.

However, the mental component of human male sexual satisfaction (the animal dominance component), is much more difficult to satisfy. It consists essentially of a male needing to be convinced that he is the most worthwhile and sexually desirable male in his whole communal group. And if and when any female in his communal group should want to engage in sexual activity, he would want her first to choose him to engage in that activity with her. And if and when he had had sufficient of that type of activity, he might generously pass her off onto one or another of his preferred lieutenants. All that would work just fine for him, and perhaps not too badly for his preferred lieutenants, but other males in the communal group would be left quite wanting.

The remaining sexually wanting males, rarely or never being chosen for sexual activity with desiring females, might choose to bargain with one or another female to provide sexual relief for himself in return for resources, be it money, food, services, or other. And as sure as the sun will rise tomorrow, one or another female will be found who will accommodate his wishes, but usually in return for a significant price. And while the resulting sexual activity may satisfy the physical component of his sex drive, it does not very well satisfy his mental component. By having to pay for her sexual services, it becomes increasingly obvious to him that he is not the most highly desirable male in the group, and consequently his drive to prove himself more sexually adequate becomes rather compelling. But not understanding the basic source of his discomfort, he may try to satisfy it by repeated prostitution, and thus he may become more or less consumed by sexual addiction.

On the female side of the ledger, text books state that what females want primarily from a male in a conjugal type of relationship is "status and resources". She thus is likely to choose as her breeding partner the male that can best supply these items, since they will be most important in the subsequent raising of her children. And it normally does not matter much to her if she has to share that male's available resources with another female, as long as her personal share is sufficiently generous. Thus she might prefer to engage in a bigamous relationship with a male of high status and large resources, in preference to a monogamous relationship with a male of lesser status and fewer resources.

Bigamous relationships are discouraged in our western world, chiefly, it would seem, because of traditional societal disapproval. Nevertheless, many women are content to let their husband have a girlfriend on the side, provided (1) that he continues to provide adequately for his wife's reasonable needs, and (2) that he keeps public knowledge of his girlfriend very quiet so that his wife does not get harassed publicly for letting such a situation exist. Public harassment leads rather quickly to divorce.

On a wholly practical basis, let me suggest that most marriages in the western world are undertaken on the basis that "if you will agree to do this for me, then I will agree to do that for you". It constitutes a negotiated contract whose permanence depends upon an evaluation of continued satisfactory performance on the part of the other. To me, that seems to differ only in detail from a similarly agreed upon contract between a prostitute and her client. And both of those, however you dress them up with considerations of relative permanence, seem to constitute basically one or another form of prostitution. The underlying consideration of the newly married female is usually "when you no longer please me, I will be out the door". And of the male, it is often "when you no longer please me, I will start looking for a second female". And supporting those allegations is the well known fact that half of all first marriages undertaken in the western world ultimately end in divorce.

But if the legal wife satisfies well the needs of her chosen husband, then he is normally not much inclined to seek a second female. And if he is adequately taken care of by his wife, he will be inclined in turn to make a rather large effort to satisfy well all of her needs. Such a happy monogamous relationship has been called "a covenant relationship", and if pursued diligently, it becomes unusually comfortable and long lasting. In times of difficulty, if one partner should deviate temporarily from acceptable conduct, the relationship remains highly capable of repair should the other partner continue diligently both to assess and supply the reasonable needs of the deviant one. A major bonus for this type of relationship is the fact that one might expect children reared by a couple in covenant relationship to experience more love, and to suffer less trauma and other harmful treatment, than would children reared by parents more often in conflict, as would be expected if their relationship were based more on a prostitution type of format.

Saint Augustine, the Catholic Faith, and Evolution by Natural Selection: It is time for a reassessment of faith

The Catholic principles of faith established by Saint Augustine were based chiefly on interpretations of the Genesis story of Adam and Eve. The more recent understanding of the origin of the human species through evolution by natural selection from more primitive types indicates the need for a reassessment of the position of mankind in the modern and future world.

In her book, "Adam, Eve, and the Serpent", Elaine Pagels (1988) outlines the life of Jesus and the nature of his teachings, particularly as they related to such factors as sexuality, marriage, procreation, and celibacy. She indicates that for more than a millennium, Jews had taught that "the purpose of marriage, and therefore of sexuality, was procreation". Prostitution, homosexuality, abortion, and infanticide practices all "contradicted Jewish custom and law". Jewish custom banned sexual acts not conductive to procreation, and the impurity laws even prohibited marital intercourse except at times most likely to result in conception. These attitudes were supposed to have been derived from the ancient accounts of creation, specifically the biblical story of Adam and Eve.

The teachings of Jesus did not completely oppose sexual activity, but he did praise "those who have made themselves eunuchs for the sake of the Kingdom of Heaven". Specifically, Jesus endorsed the rejection both of marriage and of procreation in favor of "voluntary celibacy, for the sake of following him into the new age".

Years after the crucifixion of Jesus, the disciple Paul carried the principle of celibacy much further. Paul considered even the most casual sexual encounter to be "a form of bondage". All sexual activity was to be avoided so as not to distract from the proclamation of the gospel in preparation for the coming of the Kingdom of Heaven.

Within a century of Paul's death, Pagels indicates that ascetic versions of Jesus' message were being spread rapidly. She relates stories of early Christian preachers "attempting to persuade men and women to 'undo the sin of Adam and Eve' by choosing celibacy", which disrupted the traditional order of family, village, and city life, and encouraged believers to reject ordinary family life for the sake of Christ.

Many other Christians protested sharply. Such radical asceticism was not, they argued, the primary meaning of Jesus' gospel, and they simply ignored the more radical implications of what Jesus and Paul taught. Two major schools of thought emerged concerning the proper role of sexuality in Christian life. One considered that marriage, for Christians as well as for Jews, was a positive act, involving "cooperation with God's work of creation". But it was still considered second best to celibacy, with sexuality, even within marriage, being best limited to specific acts intended for procreation. The alternate school of Christian thought, on the other hand, endorsed procreation within marriage, not only as normal, but even as the sanctified, preferred course of Christian life.

Pagels describes the severe persecution of believing Christians under the hand of the Roman rulers, specifically death to any and all who called themselves "Christian", and who thus chose death rather than to sacrifice to the Roman emperor's "divine spirit". Finally in the third century, as we all know, the emperor Constantine changed Roman policy from one of persecuting Christians to protecting and favoring them very generously. By this time, there were very many differing versions of Christianity being practiced throughout the then civilized world, and efforts soon were initiated to institutionalize and strengthen them by joining them into a common doctrine and discipline. Non-conformists and dissidents were considered dangerous to the movement, and efforts were made by orthodox leaders increasingly to suppress them one by one, and increasingly as necessary by the use of imperial force.

Pagels describes in detail many of the arguments of various writers and preachers supporting and opposing the various controversial doctrines, culminating in the fourth century theologian

Augustine (later to become Saint Augustine) in controversy with such other Christian leaders as John Chrysostom, the Donatists, the Pelagians, and especially Julian of Eclunam. Augustine would eventually, in the end, transform traditional Christian teaching on freedom, on sexuality, and on sin and redemption, for future generations of Christian believers. All of the opposing leaders, in fact, became labeled eventually as "heretics", and were removed from influence within the official Roman Catholic church.

All such early arguments on sexuality were, in fact, based directly on differing personal interpretations of the Genesis story of Adam and Eve. Augustine argued that through a deliberate act of will, Adam and Eve in fact changed the structure of the universe: that their single willful act permanently corrupted human nature as well as nature in general: and that in our present state of moral corruption, what we need spiritually is divine grace, and what we need practically is external authority and guidance from both church and state. Julian, on the other hand, argued that neither death nor sexual desire troubled Adam and Eve in Paradise, for both death and desire were "natural", and that God made nothing evil: that the "death as punishment for sin" as outlined in Genesis, was considered as a moral and spiritual death only, and not a physical death: that God gave to every human being what he gave to Adam, - the power to choose one's own moral destiny, the power to choose either the spiritual way of life or spiritual destruction.

Augustine's whole argument seems to result chiefly from his questionable but insistent claim that man cannot control his own sex drive, that a man's sex drive is, in fact, in control of him. And Augustine's own confessed background and writings indicate clearly to me that he personally was moderately or severely addicted to sexual desire. The other writers on Christian sexuality seem to offer nothing to suggest in any way that they were similarly addicted. They would seem all to be capable of controlling their respective sexual desires quite adequately. And to my simple understanding, that is the most vital and critical feature of the whole continuing controversy. Those differences in interpretation of the ancient biblical story in Genesis, moreover, have had extremely important implications on other facets of modern life, such as the question, "Is mankind capable of governing himself? Or does he need to be governed by an external authority?" The Roman Catholic Church for the past sixteen centuries has believed and claimed that we, in fact, do need to be governed by outside authority. Whether or not that external governing was in fact necessary, well, that is now history. I am arguing herein that now is the time for a reassessment of the proper role of mankind in the present and future world.

All of the critical arguments presented above were based, as stated earlier, on various interpretations of the ancient Genesis story of Adam and Eve. Certainly in this day and age, one just cannot believe in a literal interpretation of that story. Especially with the more recent understanding of evolution by natural selection and the realization that in fact mankind has evolved as a species over a very long time from more primitive types, one is tempted to classify the Adam and Eve story in the same category as the Hansel and Gretel story, or with Ali Baba and the Forty Thieves. However, the latter stories would seem to have originated mostly for entertainment value, whereas the Adam and Eve story was more likely told to illustrate some particular point of view. In fact, nobody was sitting on a camp stool way back then with a tape recorder in his hand, recording for us the beginnings of mankind. Such ancient stories as we know them have originated in the imagination of one person's brain, and have no doubt been molded continuously through time by verbal retelling.

As I have postulated in previous articles, we have a brain made up of several anatomical modules. Among those, one part handles conscious thought, another handles unconscious thought, a third (the so-called reptilian brain) handles our sexuality, and so on. We have some appreciation of what is going on in our conscious brain, but not so for the unconscious module. Let us suppose that accumulated knowledge is either stored in the unconscious brain, or is readily available to it. And suppose that that module works diligently trying to solve problems that may be bothering us. We would normally be completely unaware of all this. And when a promising solution to one of our vexing problems gets arrived at, it would shoot the information over to our conscious brain, and all of a sudden we would get "a bright idea". We might claim and believe that

God had just spoken to us. And he is a very wise God who loves us beyond all our expectations. And part of the information that went into that decision may actually have been something that we read previously, possibly even from the Holy Bible.

Why do we have to postulate an external God to explain such bright ideas? Or for any other reason? And if there really were an external God out there, how should we attempt to understand the physical nature of all that? Now in true scientific tradition, I will admit that the above suggestions may possibly be all wrong. But I have sincere faith in them, and only time and further understanding will indicate ultimately whether or not my faith was well placed.

Capitalists and Socialists:
Opponents who need Each Other

A relationship similar to the "predator-prey" relationship in animals is suggested. A preferred situation would be less indoctrination into "isms", and an increased focus on an intermediate position.

In the field of wildlife biology, a lot of study has gone into an understanding of what is known as "the predator-prey relationship". The phenomenon is present in the relationship between owls and field mice, between wolves and caribou, between grouse and goshawks, and so on, and so on. And there is a balance between the two related groups, such that when one side gets the upper hand, it lives at a disadvantage, whereas its related group enjoys an advantage, and vice versa. When grouse are plentiful, there is increased competition between them for food, which for them is a disadvantage. At the same time, the high population of grouse provides more food than usual for the goshawks, which helps them increase their population.

But when the population of goshawks increases, there is more predation on the population of grouse, and grouse numbers decrease. The goshawks then have fewer grouse to feed on, and they suffer population losses. But then when grouse numbers decrease, the remaining grouse have an easier time finding food, so they prosper and their numbers tend to grow again. And so a varying "biological balance" is established. The goshawks need the grouse as they are mostly their only supply of food, whereas the grouse need the goshawks to keep their population numbers within reasonably bounds. True, it is a deadly game, but in the end, it seems to work out quite well.

A somewhat similar but differing relationship exists between males and females of any species. With humans, if we were to destroy most all males one by one for their terrible behavior, the females would have a more difficult time providing a living for themselves and their children, and in producing sufficient replacement children with the few males left. But on the other hand, without females, the males just could not replace their numbers at all. So again, the situation is one in which males really need females, and females really need males, just to perpetuate their species. The ratio of males to females may vary, perhaps quite a lot in some circumstances, but there is an essential balancing feature between the two, just as with grouse and goshawks.

And getting finally to the case of capitalists and socialists, there again we have two groups with distinctly different interests that are at competition with each other. I tend to associate the poor with socialism, and the rich with capitalism. That doesn't always hold as a firm rule, as you would well know, but there is a distinct tendency that way. In our case, the two groups are not different species, but are certainly different cultural types within the one species. And whereas we mostly would like to encourage the growth of the in-betweens (the middle class), there seems to be a strong natural tendency for "the rich to get richer, and the poor to get poorer".

And again, I feel strongly that there is a necessary balance between the two, the capitalists need the labor of the poor, and the poor need financial support from the rich. Persons brought up in the culture of the poor tend to support the attitudes of the poor throughout life, whereas persons brought up in the culture of the rich tend to support the attitudes of the rich throughout their life. But now, if we should all choose to increase the proportion of those in the flimsy "middle class", well then, how would we go about doing all that ??

I like to compare the attitudes of the rich on the one hand, and the poor on the other hand, with differing attitudes toward religious belief. We all have our own religious beliefs, with which we have had to struggle, to choose, and to adopt as part of our way of living. And once we have settled finally on one reasonably comfortable way of approaching problems in life, we do not take too kindly to someone trying to change the very way that we have chosen, after much struggle, to live. And that, I feel, is what a lot of "social reformers" are trying to do. They may speak most convincingly, but let me be honest about it, I hesitate seriously to adopt uncritically any messages that they are trying to put out. And although they may conscript a great many converts across Canada, well, there are a lot of Roman Catholics across Canada, too! But try to convince a Canadian of the Protestant persuasion to join the Roman Catholic faith, and you will not have a whole lot of "takers". Maybe a few here and there, but not many!

And so I like to approach the problem from the basic starting point. I do not like young people being indoctrinated into anything. I like to push for freedom in learning, freedom from indoctrination, freedom to pursue study in any field to which an active curiosity might attract that particular person. I believe sincerely that persons raised in that way would be more responsible and make better decisions than those raised to accept the indoctrinated beliefs of others. And so, in the song with the chorus, "Life is o so difficult, things are really bad; surely there is a better way!", the verse that I have chosen to offer at this point is, I feel, quite an appropriate one to add to that familiar old song that we all are singing. That's the way I see it, anyway!!

Advice to a Teenager:
Helpful suggestions on "How to grow up"

Teenagers should increasingly try to make and carry out their own decisions following meditation, resisting forces of indoctrination commonly pushed by many other well meaning members of society.

I think a person at your stage of life would be wise to try more and more to insist on making his or her own decisions. Other people will always be telling you what you should do, and what you should not do, but you would be advised to take that only as advice. Listen to what they have to say, not so much as to what they think you should be doing, but paying careful attention to the actual reasons why they think their choice is the best one. You may have to ask them, why? why? why?, and they may have very good reasons for their choice, which you might be very wise to consider. But your final choice should be your own, made by you, after meditating on all the relevant data. And the principle of always doing exactly the opposite of what others suggest is usually not a good idea. That way, they still control your behavior, but in reverse.

Often, the wise choice really is to do exactly what they suggest, but if and only if it makes good sense to you. And at other times, your best choice will be to ignore their advice completely. Arguing with them in such a case is often necessary to fully comprehend their reasons. But your final choice after considering all such relevant advice should be such as not to keep you awake at night. Any later feeling that you were coerced into making a choice against your better senses, will give rise to a very uncomfortable situation with which you will have to live.

Sure, you will make some bad decisions from time to time, and you personally will have to accept responsibility for having made them. But if they were really honest decisions, you will learn from your mistakes, and you should not feel guilty. And with each decision carried through to completion, your skill and confidence in making critical decisions will grow. And that, in my humble opinion, is the proper attitude and method by which teenagers like yourself can most effectively "grow up". That's the way I see it, anyway!

The Development of Mind, Community, Social Conflict, and the Ethics of Love and Freedom: As seen through the principles of evolutionary biology

Many of the traditional "highly mysterious" features of human life that are considered by religious believers to be under the sole control of GOD, become not so mysterious when they are examined through the principles of evolutionary biology.

Persons with a religious orientation often "pray to GOD" concerning "the great mysteries of life", such as the origin of life, the varying strength of faith in their leaders, the role of sex, evil and sin in daily life, the why of the great drive for love relationships, and so on and so on. These factors are mostly complete mysteries to persons versed primarily in theology, and consequently are mostly ascribed to being controlled by their imaginary "GOD". But such considerations are not always so mysterious when they are examined from the viewpoint of evolutionary biology.

For biologists, the human species has evolved slowly over millennia from more primitive types by the process of natural selection. For most believers, mankind was created by GOD in the order of six or seven thousand years ago. These differing explanations concerning the origin of mankind have a history of angry conflict, which is still hotly active in parts of North America even today.

These two conflicting explanations may possibly be reconciled if we realize that most believers consider the human person to be essentially a "spirit" or a "soul", and the human body to be only "the house" in which the human spirit lives. There could perhaps be some agreement that the present form of the human body has evolved over millennia from more primitive types, whereas the "spirit nature" of mankind could have developed into its recognizable condition only as recently as the past few thousand years.

All vertebrates essentially have an anatomical brain, which we consider regulates such animal functions as breathing, digestion, circulation, and so on. The part of the brain that regulate the sex drive for reproduction is commonly known as the "reptilian brain", or perhaps "the reptilian part of the brain".

Recent reports of experiments conducted by psychologist Timothy D. Wilson of Virginia, and by neurologist Antonio Damasio of Iowa have suggested that the brain function of thinking may be separated further as one part coming from a conscious component of the human brain while another part comes from an unconscious component of that same brain. While the unconscious function of the human brain may have evolved a very long time ago, we can perhaps postulate that the conscious component of the same brain may have evolved sufficiently well to have begun to function as such only as recently as a few thousand years ago. Presumably, this additional planning capacity would have provided for a considerably improved capacity for human survival, such that it would have been favored by natural selection. And we might expect this increased level of survival to have resulted in a relatively rapid evolutionary development of our conscious brain capacity.

The battle between the good (the righteous component) and the bad (the evil, or devil component) of the human brain may possibly have resulted from an internal struggle for overall control between the conscious mind (good) and the unconscious mind (not always so good).

The unconscious mind, which seems to be the ancient "quick and dirty" component of the brain, would be the first to answer the call for a decision on action to be taken following a particular challenge. The conscious mind, being much slower, but probing much deeper into the more distant future, could in time perhaps come up with a much wiser solution to that challenge, particularly following a period of serious meditation. When that wiser answer eventually gets arrived at, its deliverance may coincide with what is recognized by believers as "The Holy Spirit". The Holy Spirit is a very wise internal voice ranging from very softly spoken to quite strongly spoken, and it is considered by believers to be coming "directly from GOD". If its expression is controlled by a genetic capacity which varies somewhat from one person to another, then that genetic capacity might explain its variable expression more credibly than the depth of faith entertained by the particular person involved.

It may be possible that the unconscious mind could "learn" from the decisions of the conscious mind, and in time come up with wiser decisions on its own. This idea may be consistent with the "religious conversion" phenomenon, whereas a decision may possibly be made to transfer ultimate control of the thinking process over from the unconscious brain to the conscious brain. And as that individual subsequently "learns more righteousness" from the teachings of his/her religious advisors, then his/her unconscious brain would become more and more religiously oriented in "the ways of GOD", and the person's quick response behavior would become more and more "GOD-like".

With the early shifting of life style from that of a nomadic nature into that of small communities, the greatest common wisdom at that early stage of civilization may have been to follow the teachings and directions of the community's most respected leader. The tendency to want to serve one particularly wise leader "unto death" might have had strong survival value for the community as a whole, even if it should require the sacrifice of valuable individual members of the community. Thus the tendency for this servant-type of behavior might well have been strengthened over the generations by natural selection.

The strength of the sex drive for reproduction would already have evolved to a very strong force in pre-human types, and would have been maintained strong in human types since those with a low reproductive drive would have been at a direct disadvantage in natural selection. A moderating influence on sex drive for reproduction would have been provided by the collective action of other members of the community in providing punishment for expressions of the drive so strongly expressed as to become a burden on the rest of the community.

It seems that, without exception, all humans crave an intimate and trusting relationship with at least one other person. When the chosen other person is of the opposite gender, the satisfying of this craving would normally lead to a greater production of offspring than if the craving were weaker, non-existent, or unsatisfied. This provides a strong selection pressure for such craving, and is no doubt the simple explanation for that very strong craving instinct that has evolved in all of us. With or without the ready presence of such a trusting friend, most strong religious believers turn to "their imaginary GOD" to serve as an always present and very trusting friend. Their imaginary GOD can be a most powerful force in their lives, even more trustworthy than any live human could be expected to be, but perhaps somewhat less helpful than a trusted spouse might be in arriving at a wise solution to a particularly difficult personal problem.

Along with our craving for a trusting and intimate relationship with at least one other person, we seem to experience a great hungry need to receive love, and hopefully a reciprocal wish to extend love. Almost without exception, religious believers consider "this mysterious" phenomenon to be of a "GOD-given nature". That perhaps is a very convenient way to describe a very strong universal instinct that is in reality mostly under genetic control. Increased male reproduction would be expected to follow should a particular male become highly attractive to females, and that attraction would certainly be strengthened by a high level of expressed love, including generosity. Effective reproduction by females would be increased should the female express "love" to a particular male sufficient for him to want to stay around to help raise any resulting children. Thus, there is a strong survival value associated in general with a greater expression of love, and particularly if that expression is directed toward a trusted spouse with whom a very intimate relationship has been established. And when a characteristic has both survival value and is at least partly under genetic control, it gets strengthened generation by generation by the evolutionary process of natural selection.

The conscious component of the brain is most likely the major motivator in such expressed love, and thus a marked increase in the thinking capacity of the conscious brain might well result generation after generation from natural selection as a result of this one particular factor alone, and that would be in addition to the effects of any and all other complementary factors.

The reason for our instinctive drive for increased personal freedom is not quite so obvious. However, it is possible that, whereas the drive to serve a strong and trusted wise leader has survival value when population numbers are low, there may be a switch over to a higher survival value for the urge towards personal freedom when population numbers and population density are increased. That might possibly explain why the ethic toward personal freedom seems now to be evolving stronger, generation by generation.

Trust, and the Biblical Tithe
Not all receivers are equally worthy

Tithing is a time honored biblical tradition. However, much of what is contributed ends up as being of little value in promoting "the Lord's work". An example is offered of what may be a better way to tithe.

When we ask others what they consider to be the most serious of the root problems in the world today, they well might indicate the absence of honesty, the lack of trust, routine sexual abuse, and too much effort by a few strongly to coerce the many. There have been too many examples of all of these throughout history, but it seems that today, for whatever reason, we seem to be experiencing a virulent epidemic of all of the above.

The feeling is rampant throughout society that mankind is doomed, that we are headed for extinction as a species, and that there is just no reasonable hope for a brighter future. With such feelings of hopelessness, too many people seem to have given up the challenge of trying to make the world a better place in which to live. "What is the use?", one is often asked. It is sad to realize that such people have chosen, apparently, to "get what they can out of life while the getting is still good".

While the ranks of such a category of people is bulging at the seams, not all of us are content to accept what seems to many to be "the inevitable". There are still today many "very good" people in the world, just as there have always been. It is just that they are not always recognizable. They tend to be somewhat humble people, who continue to perform good deeds diligently without a lot of fanfare, and who trust that, in the end, their efforts will be rewarded. There are many such people wherever we look, (many, but perhaps not enough). However, we often fail to recognize them as role models, or to learn of their valuable activities.

People tend to reflect rather closely the kind of behavior that they have observed as being "successful" for other people, especially the behavior of those persons who they more or less admire. And this pattern of behavior becomes established most firmly during a person's young formative years. By early maturity, such behavior patterns tend to be rather firmly established, often lasting firmly throughout a full lifetime. No amount of preaching in the whole world is likely to make much improvement in the behavior of such a person while their outlook on life remains essentially positive.

Only at a time of significant mental crisis do established behavior patterns come under serious scrutiny. The thought in times of crisis typically becomes, "Where did I go wrong?" "How do I have to change my life so that this type of thing does not happen again?" And at such a time, a person "searches" for a more promising pattern of behavior upon which to pattern their future development. Where can such a person find an example of such a promising pattern of behavior? Who will serve as a worthwhile role model?

At such a time of searching, a person becomes most vulnerable to the teachings of "pushy" people, such as evangelistic preachers. Such preachers are certainly highly visible, and they often try to intensify any feeling of crisis in others by preaching "Hell and damnation!!". Sometimes their impassioned pleas result in a very significant improvement in the life of the searching person. But just as often, the obvious hypocrisy of the preacher does a most effective job of poisoning the healing message, in variations ranging from a request to "buy some of my magic snake oil" on to "contribute as generously as you can to keep this program on the air". Such poisoning does little to establish trust in anyone, and is not only most effective in staining severely the reputation of all religious "do-gooders", but also raises serious questions concerning the integrity of the many "miraculous" promises of traditional religion.

Not to suggest that evangelistic preachers are the only bad examples. Such people as politicians, lawyers, corporation executives, used car salesmen, and even some medical practitioners have, as a class, been recognized as being in a position where it is prudent to offer them very little in the way of trust, and similarly to expect little of them in the way of honesty. Such naivety would almost certainly result sooner or later in disappointment and what may be called "moral anger". And such anger is often directed at society in general for letting such happenings go on unpunished. It is neither a happy nor a promising situation!!

While preachers like to "tell" us all about honesty, trust, and the love of others, "preaching" is not usually the most effective way to get the message across. "Showing the way" seems always to be more effective than mere "telling about it". They say that one picture is often more effective than a thousand words, and while that still is only a bunch of words, the message is probably quite true.

In March of 2002, I met a girl at her 14th birthday party. She seemed to be a highly intelligent person, sharp, alert, attentive, and I learned that she was trilingual (fluent in English, and in French, and in Spanish). She reportedly had been at the top of her class in Grade six, again in Grade seven, and was now in grade eight at public school. This was in spite of the fact that her parents were divorced, and that she was living under quite limited financial conditions. This seemed to me to be a grand opportunity!!

She had learned some about computers in school, and was handling e-mail with some friends through her "hotmail" account at the public library. The first thing I did was to buy a new iMac computer and inkjet printer as a surprise gift for her personal use. We opened a bank account for her at the local bank, and I began depositing money into her account online each week through the Internet. I did not tell her how to spend the money. It was hers, to do with as she chose.

My pension income during retirement is just under $50,000 per year. An honest "biblical tithe" would be between $96 and $97 per week, and so my weekly transfer to her account has been $100 per week from then until now, and continuing, supported by a series of post-dated cheques. That financial support is given to her through an extension of "trust", with the understanding that if she wishes ever to repay, that she should forward the money similarly on to another young person whom she judges to be "worthy".

During the summer of 2002, my young friend has gone horseback riding, has bought herself a bicycle, has learned the skills rather adequately of driving an automobile, and has experienced the thrill of several sessions of pilot training, flying a Cessna 152 aircraft. During the school year, we are keeping in contact through e-mail, and making plans for next summer.

I feel personally that my financial contribution (tithe) is being very well focused on enriching the development of a very promising young person. I feel strongly that the development of one more highly capable adult, one who may possibly become an effective world leader in the field of her choice, is a much more hopeful way to improve conditions of mankind in the world than by trying to pull everyone up to an "average level" "by their boot straps". That's the way I see it, anyway!!

A Second Look at Eugenics and the Human Race:
A possible block upon which to build our chosen future

From our very earliest memories, we have all been indoctrinated in the belief that "All men were created equal". That attitude toward life, when implemented in a society with low population numbers, has been highly successful in building a strong and vibrant society with unusually superior intellectual and technological achievements. The idea that we are all born equal, however, is open to question when considered from a truly technical standpoint. A purist might argue that men were not "created" at all, but in fact have "evolved through natural selection". Rather than being sidetracked by that argument, let us agree that we are all born with a distinctive package of genetic endowments. Only identical twins are destined to be born really equal, and even there, differences in development of the fetus during gestation cause even identical twins at birth to differ in minor detail.

Biologists generally agree that both inherited and developmental effects contribute to the differences that we can see or can measure between individuals. Many studies have attempted to measure the relative contributions of these two factors in determining the ultimate expression of particular personal traits. For some traits, such as eye color, the genetic component is by far the stronger factor. For other traits, such as maybe body weight at maturity, the developmental effects are relatively much stronger. In the end, a very wide range of variation has been found to exist between the contributions of these two factors, but it would seem that in every case, both factors make at least some minor contribution to the final expression.

As a scientist with professional training and decades of experience in plant breeding, I recognize possibly better than most the potential genetic improvement that could possibly be made in the human race through some elementary manipulation of ongoing breeding patterns. Patterns designed to make significant genetic improvements over generations are very easy to outline on paper, but their possible implementation in the actual lives of people in our society would be quite another matter. Nevertheless, some effort along this line has already been carried out in California with the "Repository for Germinal Choice", more commonly known as "The Nobel Prize Winners Sperm Bank". And also, genetic progress is currently underway in avoiding the incidence of some inherited defects through ongoing human genetic counseling.

Aside from inherited defects, one consideration that is perhaps not well appreciated by many interested persons is how frequently a factor that confers a significant benefit through natural selection in one particular environment may in fact be neutral or even detrimental in another environment. A simple to understand example is dark skin color in areas of high sunlight versus light skin color in areas of lesser sunlight. Local deficiencies versus adequacies in nutrition is another possible case in point.

Physical capabilities are routinely measured by such factors as performance in athletic competition and in other physically demanding ventures. And natural selection perhaps responds by favoring those of greater ability. This selection may or may not improve very slightly the average physical ability of persons over generations, but it does at least tend to maintain a high level of performance by culling out those mutations that arise now and then that tend to decrease overall physical performance.

When we consider possible genetic improvements in such factors as mental ability, we tread on much shakier grounds. One prime problem is the difficulty in measuring mental performance with any degree of accuracy. And we must keep in mind that planned genetic improvement comes only following some accurate assessment of only the genetic component contributing to mental performance. But mental performance is very highly affected by developmental factors also. A child with average mental capacity can, on the one hand, exhibit near genius performance if prepared extremely well, or, on the other hand, can perform pitifully poorly if his/her upbringing was hopelessly inadequate. That is similar to trying to compare the production capacity of a number of cultivars of tomatoes in a very weedy and highly variable garden plot. You can measure accurately the actual production of each cultivar, but you will have no faith that the results thus obtained reflect the genetic potential of the particular cultivars in question. It is only when you grow the plants under comparable growing conditions that measured production will mean anything. And the cultivar that does best under one level of care is not always the best one when grown under different conditions of care.

Similarly, evaluation of a child's mental potential might best be determined when all children are raised and educated under conditions as optimal as possible. That particular consideration would argue strongly for the provision of highly adequate conditions for growth and enlightened education for those children considered to be the most promising. Not only do they represent the best potential breeding parents for the next generation, but many will also be the top future leaders of society. And the better educated they are, the better job they will likely do in developing wise courses of future action, and in leading society on to greater and better things.

Another consideration causing complications in assessing human mental ability is the fact that performance in mental ability is a very complex thing, made up of an almost unlimited number of facets. That being the case, the task of designing theoretical schemes of breeding for the successful simultaneous improvement of several genetic factors calls for a much greater level of expertise. That level of expertise in breeding for simultaneous improvement over many difficult-to-measure factors is most likely available best from professionals trained and experienced in the breeding of domestic animals such as cattle, chickens, swine, race horses and working dogs.

The proposition of implementing artificial patterns of breeding of real live people to achieve ultimate genetic improvement will almost certainly horrify many of us. The very word "eugenics" may roll up visions of Hitler and WWII, of the holocaust, of mercy killing, and of all the historical controversies related to human abortion. Nevertheless, with the better present understanding of the science of genetics, of advanced statistical methods, of artificial insemination, of techniques of safe sex, of sex psychology, of child adoption procedures, of surrogate motherhood, of gene pool preservation, and generally of effective animal breeding, it might be wise, if we can subdue the reaction of horror down to a more comfortable level, to give the proposition of eugenics for the human race a serious second look.

Before any attempt is made to implement grandiose patterns of breeding humans for genetic improvement, I believe that a responsible discussion of the whole proposition should be encouraged widely and with depth throughout society. We should recognize immediately that most people will likely object to the whole idea, and will want to maintain "the old traditional ways". And that is fine. Any attempts at improvement should be on a strictly voluntary and knowledgeable basis. And I believe further that all such attempts should be financed on a voluntary basis, rather than by asking objecting taxpayers to foot the bill.

Most likely, we are not yet nearly ready to implement any kind of direct action, but at least we should open our minds to a consideration and a responsible discussion in detail of the possible ramifications of the basic proposition. Only after that might it be wise to consider whether to proceed slowly and gingerly on from genetic counseling to something more promising further on down the road, or whether to soft pedal eugenics as an interesting idea that has arrived well ahead of its time.

The above considerations are offered boldly but seriously as possible building blocks upon which responsible people might choose the kind of society to which they would like to see our human race eventually to evolve. And only after considering all of that, if it seemed desirable, appropriate policies related to such factors as enlightened education, research, immigration, the judiciary, and so on, could be conceived, explained, and initiated, to allow those so interested to try to direct the evolution of a segment of our human race up to those peculiar and particular ends. And those segments of the population who wished to maintain "the old ways" would serve as a valid "scientific control group" for the long term "human experiment". Just think about it!!

Sexual Freedom, Sexual Abuse, and the Abortion Debate:
There can be no rights without responsibility

If we wish to exercise freedom in the area of sexual activity, we must accept certain responsibilities that go along with that chosen freedom. The pro-choice position in the abortion debate is defended.

In no area of human activity is the principle of freedom more valuable than in the exploration and exercise of sexual activity. We all have a very strong drive to explore and to experiment concerning sex. It is perhaps the most positively directed of all of our inherited behavioral characteristics. If we have a weak innate drive to explore and to experiment in the area of sex, our genes promoting those traits will be passed on to the next generation with less active force than if that innate drive were strong. That is simply a key part of our evolutionary experience, as it is with all vertebrates.

Young children find sooner or later that exploring their own genitalia becomes a matter of great interest, even an experience that provides welcomed pleasure. On their own, or possibly as encouraged by others, they normally will focus with great interest on such activity. This type of activity has, historically, been condemned rather severely by most adults (for good reason), but actually encouraged by a very few other persons (for very selfish reasons). And this is the initial point at which those severely damaging controversies related to sex that often trouble us in later life have their beginnings. And so, a very major critical question arises in the form of: "How should we react, in the world of today, when young children begin to display those sorts of activities?"

On a very personal note, I can recall only once that my mother advised me concerning such questionable activity. Motivated strongly by emotion, she warned me quietly but most firmly, "Leave women alone until after you are married!" I have meditated long and hard over that very brief item of advice. My father also seemed highly concerned about such activity, but he stoically kept his cool and never actually issued any verbal proclamations. I feel that they both wanted strongly to advise me with appropriate wisdom always to think long term before any action was taken, but neither seemed confident enough to express those feelings in actual words. Their message, nevertheless, came through loud and clear, and I feel that it was served tactfully, with great love and respect.

A very usual pattern of behavior for boys around the time of puberty is, with an increasing level of motivation, to approach girls for the purpose of sexual exploration and experimentation. That is a normal part of their sense of curiosity, their innate drive to learn. And the usual pattern of behavior for parents has been to keep their developing children completely "in the dark" about such matters, in the belief/hope that if their children know absolutely nothing about sex, that such activity will automatically be postponed until a later, more appropriate time of life.

But such beliefs/hopes are simply not supported by fact. Curiosity about sex does not arise solely from learning. Such curiosity is deeply engendered in children by natural selection (evolution), just as it is in all other higher vertebrates. I believe a much wiser approach with children is to erect no barriers to learning. By answering all of their questions briefly but honestly, they can be made aware of the pitfalls of such activities, and while offering them our best honest reasons to postpone such relations until later in life, I think it wise to let them make their own choices in such matters. If we have established with them a good level of love, trust and respect, then they are likely to make an honest, informed, personal evaluation of our reasons for postponement. Our ultimate objective should be to help them to grow voluntarily into responsible, self-confident, contributing adulthood, and for us not to have to apply force or coercion to accomplish such ends. If such force or coercion seems necessary, the parent(s) should perhaps look within themselves in order to make necessary adjustments and/or corrections.

Let me propose that children be encouraged to limit their exploration and sexual experimentation to what has been termed "outercourse", and that they be encouraged not to become involved in full

51

"sexual intercourse". If and when they should go beyond "outer-course", it would be against parental advice, and the participants would thus become personally responsible for the results of having made and carried out such decisions on their own. The parents at that point might well withdraw and meditate concerning how good or how bad a job they had done in raising their child. And their reward or punishment would thus be delivered internally, through such meditations.

Let me propose further that boys, when motivated to explore with girls in areas related to sex, would be most wise to keep continually fully cognizant of the wishes, both spoken and implied, of their female partner. To build and to maintain a good level of trust with your partner, and ultimately with society in general, it is imperative to realize that "no!" means "no!". and not "maybe". Any tendency to inflict coercion or force upon a female to accomplish your own selfish ends will immediately shatter any trust that she and others may have extended toward you. And remember that trust, once broken, is extremely difficult to rebuild. Further. I believe that repeated attempts by a male to inflict such coercion or force upon one or more females should be handled with sharply increased levels of severity for each infraction, and that females tantalizing males for sexual purposes should similarly be dealt with in an effective way.

When full sexual intercourse is engaged in, either voluntarily or otherwise, pregnancy sometimes results. In many cases, the female evaluates this as reward for good behavior, and she becomes most pleased. In other cases, she may evaluate it as punishment for bad behavior, and she is not pleased at all! In fact, she may wish not to carry on the pregnancy to birth. With modern medical techniques, it is possible to have the pregnancy terminated easily and without undue risks to her physical health. Within our society, however, there is currently a very hot controversy concerning the question of human abortion. One point of view holds that it is basically the right of the woman to choose whether or not to have an abortion (pro-choice), while the other holds that life begins at conception, and that aborting a pregnancy constitutes an act of murder inflicted upon another human being (pro-life). And then the question becomes, "How does one reconcile these two directly opposing points of view?"

First of all, it is simply incorrect to claim that "life begins at conception". Both the egg cell and the sperm cell are quite alive before their union takes place, and they both remain quite alive during the process of fertilization (plants) and of conception (animals). Essentially, it is a process whereby a unit of life with a single complement of genetic material per cell (an egg) is joined with a second unit of life which also contains a single complement of genetic material (a mobile sperm), and the two fuse together to form a unit of life with a double complement of genetic material (a zygote).

This zygote then begins to grow and to divide, first into two cells, then into four, and so on. Through a series of steps known as "embryogenesis", it becomes first what is called a "blastocyst", then an "embryo", and then later into what is called a "fetus". At no time during the course of this development would it be proper to call it a "baby" or an "unborn baby", any more than it would be proper to call an "acorn" a "premature oak tree". The term "unborn baby" would seem to be no more meaningful to anyone than would be the terms "unborn teenager" or "unborn senior citizen".

I consider that it would not be proper to call the final product a "baby" (a human person), until its first breath of fresh air is taken in, and the baby starts exchanging its internal supply of oxygen and carbon dioxide directly with the outside through its own lungs, as opposed to exchanging it through the umbilical cord and hence through the lungs of the mother. And if one is willing to accept this simple proposal, then one can discard, finally and definitely, the concept that abortion constitutes the killing of one human being by another human being. And then the process of abortion and/or the harvesting of stem cells from embryos becomes, from a moral point of view, no more bothersome that the surgical removal of a wart, or of a growth or tumor.

Please Note: The term "outercourse" which is used in the sixth paragraph of the above text is not original with this document, even though you might not find it in your favorite dictionary. A fuller explanation of my understanding of the term may be found in Chapter 3 of this booklet, entitled, "Adolescent Sex Education" .

Justice, For a World in Conflict:
A Lesson in Trust and Democracy

The foundation for Justice is trust, and trust plus a two-thirds majority is offered as a satisfactory way to settle disputes

I am blessed with a situation which has been diagnosed officially as "bipolar disorder". It is characterized typically by feelings of extreme sadness, down even to the point of suicide, alternating with feelings of really superior mental power and capability, where thinking speeds up, causing judgment ultimately to become impaired, and potentially to speed up even more to the point of "complete insanity".

Although such feelings are supposed typically to alternate back and forth through periods of normality, I am told that very often, afflicted persons experience only the normal and the depressed phases, and do not see much of the manic phase. On the opposite side, I am told that I demonstrate mostly the normal and manic phases, and am not too much bothered by the depression phase. Nevertheless, I did attempt suicide in 1977 by swallowing a handful of 37 tranquilizer pills (Valium) at one gulp, and then going to bed for a final sleep.

Previous to that, I was engaged to a Teresa, a girl who was a citizen of Poland living in Poland, behind the "iron curtain". We were having administrative difficulties in getting permission for her to immigrate to Canada. And in a period of frustration, I decided to go over to Poland to try to expedite matters. I went down to Halifax International Airport and purchased an air ticket to Warsaw, Poland. The next flight to Warsaw was to depart after several hours, and so I relaxed on a bench there in the airport waiting room, waiting for my flight to leave.

But I had taken the precaution of telling my older brother Eric of my plans. And while I was resting comfortably in the waiting room at the airport, Eric's sense of responsibility kicked into high gear. At his home in Berwick, he began to worry about me. He knew well of my bipolar condition, that I had had very little experience in international travel, and that I had no knowledge of the Polish language. He had experienced a lot of international travel as a career flight engineer with the Canadian Armed Forces, and he sensed strongly that his younger brother was surely headed for serious trouble.

I had drifted off to sleep at the airport, and was awakened by a kindly gentleman in the uniform of an officer of the RCMP. He asked if I was waiting for a flight, and I told him yes, I was. After only a minute or so of friendly conversation, he asked if I would mind coming in to their office there to answer a few questions. No problem! I have always trusted the RCMP. I knew them well through our local gun club, and I have found them always to be reasonable, responsible, but kindly people. They asked me please to empty my pockets and to show them what was contained therein. No problem. And after some discussion of my plans to go to Poland, and why I was going there, they told me that Eric had been worried about me, and had phoned them asking them to "check me out".

I was asked, would I mind, since my flight was not scheduled to leave for several hours, would I mind if a psychiatrist asked me some questions. Well, I guess I didn't really mind, if they thought it was necessary. So they drove me down to the Dartmouth Medical Centre, and I was interviewed first by a psychiatrist there, and then by another one called over from a hospital in Halifax. Then the RCMP officer drove me, not back to the airport as I had expected, but rather to the Nova Scotia Hospital, - a mental institution! I was given the option there of signing myself in as a voluntary patient, or of being taken in as a committed patient. As I recall, I signed myself in as a voluntary patient.

Shortly after having signed myself in to that hospital, I became quite angry, - angry at Eric, angry at the RCMP, angry at the psychiatrists, angry at everyone in general. I had been minding my own business there at that airport, bothering no one, and so on, and so on. What right had they . . . .? ?

But much later, on sober meditation, I realized that, together, they well may have saved my life, regardless of any anger on my part. Both the RCMP and those psychiatrists had done their job most adequately, and I now thank them for the gentleness with which they handled me. Later, in Berwick, I thanked Eric sincerely for having accepted responsibility for my safety. He was highly relieved to hear of my thanks. He had not been at all sure that he was doing the right thing. But he did it anyway! Out of what? Brotherly love? Eric is now deceased. But I still thank him.

Then, last Sunday evening, I had prepared a letter that I was most anxious to post right off so it would be delivered to its recipient as soon as possible. But my car had developed a serious leak in its cooling system, and it was heating up very rapidly. I knew the problem, but I really wanted to mail that letter! And only three days before, I had taken the precaution of acquiring a personal cell-phone to carry in my car, mostly just for emergencies. So I took a chance, and drove my car down to the local post office and mailed that letter. Good! Mission accomplished!

But I had pushed my luck too far. On the way home, I stopped at a traffic light at one of the town's main intersections, and the car refused to go from there. I began to worry, and to experience feelings of panic starting to rise up. Over the years, I had spent a total of more than two years confined inside mental institutions, and I surely did not want to be taken back to any of those awful places again! But what else can they do with people who are exhibiting high levels of panic? With such thoughts, my level of panic only grew stronger. Oh, no! No! And then, suddenly, I remembered my newly acquired cell-phone!

I had not used my cell-phone even once since acquiring it, but I had been shown how it worked. After some fumbling in learning how to turn it on, and after a few tries at getting it to dial out, I succeeded in contacting my favorite nephew. He operates an automobile wrecking service under the name of "Lindsay Milne's Roadside Assistance". I have always trusted Lindsay. I explained my situation to him and asked him, "What should I do?" He answered confidently, "Just wait! I'll be there shortly!". And immediately my level of panic began to subside! Lindsay was coming! Everything would be okay now. And I sat in my car at the intersection with the car's 4-way flashers flicking on and off. And I waited, patiently. Everything would be all right now. Lindsay was coming!

After 15 or 20 minutes, I saw through the car's foggy wind-shield the red lights of Lindsay's wrecking truck backing up to the front of my car. I was no longer alone, alone to face the difficulty which, I had to admit, was caused by my own impaired judgment. But that difficulty had the potential of causing me to be hauled away once again to a mental hospital, a place that I had learned to hate! It had been one of those unfortunate times of panic when I had felt that I really, really, right then, needed a friend, one that I could trust and depend upon! And I truly appreciated the fact that there had been one such person out there, and that he had answered promptly my call for help.

I had succeeded, with all the responsibility that I could muster in a time of panic, in turning my problem over to such a person. And I hoped, always, that such a person would be available to me through my cell-phone. Lindsay, on numerous occasions, had always proven most forthright and competent in answering my call. And he had come through once again! Most thankfully! And so, through personal experience, I have learned of one treatment that has been really most effective in controlling my personal brand of panic. And that is a lesson that I should never forget.

There is at least one other person in whom I have a great deal of personal trust. And that is my former common-law partner, Vivian M. Pike. My trust in her and in Lindsay lies not in the fact that they always make very wise decisions. No. They both make quite bad decisions now and then, more often than either of them would like, just as you and I and everyone else does. No, the criti-cal factor in establishing my trust in them is that I believe sincere-ly that, in crisis, any decision that either of them makes with respect to me will not be made for reasons favoring their own benefit, but will be made honestly for my own ultimate benefit, whether I per-sonally agree with that decision or not.

With my propensity for impaired judgment now and then, and realizing that I am often not aware of when and if my judgment may have become impaired, I have resolved to at least try to be obedient to whatever requests that either Lindsay or Vivian make of me, whether I agree with them at the time or not. And if I disagree seriously with the request of either one of them, we will ask the other for an opinion. And a two-thirds majority will settle the matter. The wise course of action is, I believe, that if they agree with each other, and even if I disagree with both of them on that particular point, that they are to over-rule me, and should apply whatever force is necessary to cause me to submit. I believe that that is the responsible path of action for all of us. And in the end, I believe that I will want to thank them for it, if even from the grave!

Trust alone on the part of one party in the trustworthiness of a second party will resolve many situations in a satisfactory way, but it is not always enough. And a two-thirds majority alone without trust is never really enough. There must be there that real element of trust. And the higher the level of trust, the better it should all work out in the end.

On the Question of Responsibility in the Raising of Children:
Efficiency improves by accepting a higher level of responsibility

A fanciful scheme for the raising of children in a more responsible way is offered

Where successful methods of handling life's most important matters have been evolved by experience and tradition over millennia, it is unlikely that any proposed "off the cuff" changes in those methods would offer any significant improvement over the long run. One sometimes is tempted, however, to project one's imagination concerning such delicate subjects, and to see what interesting possibilities one can come up with. For example, just suppose . . . . .

"When a woman becomes pregnant, she has the free option either (1) to try to carry that pregnancy on to birth, or else (2) to have it aborted without criticism. At birth, the mother has the sole right and responsibility to choose for its future up to the point where it takes its first breath. At that exact point of development, it becomes "a human person", with all of "the rights and responsibilities pertaining thereto". And from then on until adulthood, the baby's future is to be determined by at least two outside authorities. The mother by right has the primary responsibility for the care of her baby, unless she chooses voluntarily to pass that responsibility on to another person, such as perhaps her husband, and/or the baby's biological father.

"In such a case, that secondarily responsible person would then take over primary responsibility for the baby's care, and he/she should then choose one other authority to take over secondary responsibility for the baby's care. And in such a case, the person accepting secondary responsibility might well be the baby's gestation mother and/or its biological mother, or it could be any other accepting authority, possibly even some governmentally approved

59

"regulating body", hopefully with some connection to the fraternity of medical science.

"So far so good! Our present traditional way of handling things could be made to fit fairly well into such a scheme, at least so far. But then, a three-part authority will have been set up, consisting of (1) the child, (2) a primarily responsible authority, and (3) a secondarily responsible authority. And from that point onward to adulthood, a two thirds vote will determine the child's care. The child's vote will be accepted as being essentially whatever the child seems to want. It may be over-ridden without criticism by voluntary unanimous vote of the other two.

"In particular, the situation may arise where the child is deformed, has some undesired genetic condition, cannot be raised in an acceptable way for economic reasons, or for whatever reason is just not wanted. And with the voluntary unanimous vote of two of the three responsible partners, i.e. both of the outside responsible authorities, it may then be sacrificed without criticism.

"Please note that the mother, if she does not surrender primary responsibility for the baby's care, can alone veto the sacrifice of the child, since she and the child will both be considered to have voted against any wish to have it sacrificed. But by withholding that right, she alone must accept responsibility for the care and raising of the child, assisted by whatever help she is able to attract from other persons/authorities.

Following our present traditional way of handling things, that should mean that she would normally accept primary responsibility for care of the child, assisted by the child's father. Or perhaps more traditionally (if she should so choose), the father might take over primary responsibility for the care and raising of the child, and the mother accept responsibility only for secondary care.

"Please note that for any "child of special interest", a "regulatory authority" could (if it chose to do so), provide any amount of voluntary assistance toward the raising of the child. Or, if primary or secondary responsibility for the child had been offered and had been accepted by that regulating body, then that regulating body would have one of the three votes determining the child's future.

"A most critical feature of the scheme follows. At any time during the youngster's childhood, that youngster could be forcefully sacrificed without criticism by unanimous voluntary vote of its two other responsible authorities. A set of specific "rules to follow" in such cases could well be set up by governmental authority, including (if it so chose) one all inclusive over-riding rule saying essentially "no way, no how!" But then, at some time in the distant future, that over-riding rule might well be duly amended, as supposedly can any governmental regulation, on occasion.

"Similarly, at any time during the development of the child, that child on its own might decide that it wanted to make a change of one of its two outside responsible authorities. And its own vote, plus the vote of either one of the other two authorities, would be considered sufficient to discharge that particularly unwanted authority. And hopefully the child, plus the one remaining authority, could together choose a replacement for that discharged authority.

"And at some point in its development, the developing child would most likely choose voluntarily to "graduate into adulthood". Or alternately, the two outside authorities could together make that decision, over-riding any vote of the child. And hopefully, the resulting graduation would be "a time of great celebration!" And the child would thereby be considered to be a full adult, responsible for its own care, in fact again, with "all the rights and responsibilities pertaining thereto". And both the primarily and secondarily responsible authorities would thus be "let off the hook", and they might judge the success of their efforts over the years by the level of thanks offered to them then, and/or ultimately, by the adult that they had worked (hopefully) so diligently to raise."

Please note firmly that the above ideas are offered only as fanciful possible suggestions. It would no doubt be ridiculously unwise, maybe even disastrous, to jump "with both feet" immediately into adoption of any such alternate scheme without very deep consideration. But at those special times when you might drift off into a state of fanciful dreamhood, then the above suggestions might provide somewhat of a framework upon which to weave your own fanciful thoughts.

But please note also that in times of very low population numbers, when it might be prudent to attempt to increase the number of successful births, certain specially chosen females could be (1) either impregnated by sperm from specially chosen males, or (2) implanted with specially selected embryos. The resulting babies could then have the gestation mother as the primary care giver, and a governmental authority could become the secondary care giver, and support financially the upbringing of such children to whatever degree they considered most appropriate. Suppose??

Variation in the Pattern of Human Sexual Response:
Some like it hot and some like it cold

A possible explanation for variation in patterns of human sexual behavior is suggested as resulting certainly from variation in learned determinants, but likely also affected by unknown genetically inherited factors

The very high levels of disappointment, conflict, and violence demonstrated within human sexual relationships can possibly be explained on the basis of distinctly different patterns of learning, and likely also in part by the action of one or more inherited genetic factors.

Arriving at an adequate understanding of the dynamics of human reproduction is made particularly difficult by virtue of the fact that each of us is so completely overwhelmed by almost blinding feelings of emotion related to our own personal experiences in such matters.

However, having made a great many such personal observations on the dynamics of human reproduction over the past several decades, I am now ready to offer a highly speculative tentative theory concerning the dynamics of that particular biological process.

Let us suppose that human communities throughout the world are proceeding generally to split, through the normal process of evolution by natural selection, from one fully interbreeding population into two distinctly different breeding populations. The direction in which they seem to be headed is one fully reminiscent of the rather familiar and biologically highly successful predator-prey types. Such balanced species tend to regulate and thus control their population levels by experiencing a series of population cycles in concert with negatively matching cycling of the related species. Such predator-prey arrangements are often highly stable through the long term, although often cycling wildly in the short term. It would seem that human populations may be evolving slowly in that direction, but have proceeded only a short way toward a full expression of that phenomenon.

In our particular case, the prey phase of human populations is characterized by a breeding pattern whereby male and female individuals do a series of reciprocating actions, such as birds dancing on their breeding grounds, and each further action by one is dependent upon completion of a satisfactory complementary action by the other. By a series of acceptable back and forth communications, they "get to recognize each other as one of their own type", and cooperative breeding may then proceed peacefully, and with adequate success.

The predator phase of human populations seems to be characterized by a quite different type of breeding behavior. In the predator phase of human breeding, the female tends to display herself in a provocative and tantalizing way, and the chosen male responds initially mostly on visual clues. Similarly, the male tends to display himself in a rebellious fashion, and the female responds with an attitude such as "I like sex very much, but I wouldn't let someone like you do it to me!" The male thus challenged tends to become increasingly aroused sexually, and may use increasing levels of force to achieve mating. The female "gets her jollies" from the satisfaction of having been sexually attractive enough to trigger such vigorous/violent breeding behavior on the part of her chosen male, and in advanced cases may prefer "to turn him on as fully as possible" and then refuse absolutely to have any physical sexual contact with him until a satisfactory compensatory package had been negotiated.

In many cases, it may be necessary for the female to be stimulated to full orgasm to trigger the secretion of necessary hormones and/or nutritive juices into her vagina in order for the male's sperm to survive adequately. And also, a fully rough and vigorous mating action on the part of the male may help to trigger her to ovulation, thus improving the chances of a successful encounter resulting finally in pregnancy.

It is postulated that these two types of breeding behavior are not mutually fully exclusive, but that individual persons might be capable of either type, depending in the manner in which they "were imprinted" initially into sexual activity. Thus, with a mild cooperative introduction to sexual activity, a candidate might tend to adopt the prey phase of activity, whereas with a more violent introduction to sexual activity, a candidate would tend more likely to adopt the predator phase of activity.

Further, a particular candidate may for genetic reasons tend to fall more easily into one or the other phases of breeding activity. And over time, one might expect the effect of genetic influence to increase by natural selection up to such point where genetic differences alone would determine into which phase a candidate might become imprinted.

Different species are also typically characterized by not being able to breed successfully with each other. This phenomenon has already been realize to some limited degree with our two phases of human populations. When a predator male breeds with excessive vigor/violence/rape with respect to a prey female, she gets "poisoned off" from sex to such point where she is not likely again ever to become trusting and responsive enough to a prey male to become impregnated by him. She may, however, become pregnant over and over again by repeatedly being raped by predatory males.

And when a prey male and predatory female become engaged in sexual activity, the female is rarely stimulated to orgasm, is thus not likely to become pregnant, and is generally disappointed in the male's performance. And for the prey male, the highly negative responses of the predator female are most effective in "turning off" any sexual excitement on his part. Thus, there has already developed a significant barrier to interbreeding between the two phases of the breeding pattern.

The phenomenon of Religion is intimately bound up with all of the above considerations. The "Story of Adam and Eve" of the Jewish, Christian and Islam traditions is obviously a story concocted to explain in way of fantasy such phenomena as were already being observed in then existing human populations. It would seem that the predatory phase may have been dominant in "Old Testament Times", and with the life and teachings of Jesus, a significant move toward the prey phase may have been initiated.

Jesus preached the prey phase, and some of his later followers adopted the prey phase quite firmly, while others, such as the Roman Catholic Church, preached the prey phase, but specialized in cashing in on "forgiving sinners for their trespasses" while such "forgiven sinners" continued to enjoy the predatory phase of activity. And the culmination of all this deceit has been a highly disturbed and violent human society characterized by social violence, frequent marital breakups, and a whole series of deadly wars, including the present war on terrorism, and many other (but certainly not all) past and present wars throughout the world.

When a prey female encounters an "unprimed" prey male, they together will choose the extent to which any sexual activity is allowed to work out. And it may work out very well both in the short term and in the long term, especially if they are engaged in a covenant type of love relationship.

But when the two different types of behavior cross over and come together for sexual relations, and/or when a "primed" prey male encounters a prey female in sexual union, an unsatisfactory and most disappointing predator-prey type of relationship may tend to become established.

Normally, when a prey male encounters a predator female for the first time, often following her deliberate "baiting", but possibly on his own initiative, he may be more or less adequately accommodated on the first try. But he tends to become "primed" during subsequent encounters by having to utilize both persuasion and at least a little bit of force in order to achieve his satisfaction. Thereafter, the predator female may tend on each subsequent occasion deliberately and gradually to increase the level of force he must exert in order for him to achieve internal ejaculation. And if carefully handled, she can over repeated encounters "teach" him to use more and more force against her increasing levels of resistance, resulting finally in unusually violent and satisfying encounters. She gets her ultimate satisfaction through the process of baiting and then of whipping up and experiencing the frenzied almost insane passion that he thus displays toward her otherwise rather insignificant body. But he, on the other hand, will get his delightful share of relief only if and when he has, against all of her contributed resistance, successfully ejaculated inside her vagina. In a truly monogamous type of relationship, this pattern of behavior may be mutually pleasing to both partners, provided only that the predator female maintains a reasonable cap on the level of resistance that she chooses to employ.

However, with friction in other areas of their daily life, the female may tend, even subconsciously, to want to "punish" the male by displaying unreasonable levels of resistance. She may choose repeatedly to bait him up, and then if possible, repeatedly to ward off completely his growing, insane, uncontrollable drive to "plant that baby". Such conflicts are capable of producing some degree of insanity in him, a possible brutal murder and mutilation of her body, and/or possibly other unpredictable violent types of behavior. Meanwhile, she is still getting a full measure of her personal satisfaction for having successfully denied him, and if there are any legal consequences, he will be the one most likely to have to pay.

The actual pattern of human sexual response seems to me to follow somewhat along such described lines, but may likely deviate from those on specific points. While prey and predator groups here are presented as being distinct, in reality there is surely a whole continuous range of variation between these two extremes. Some extrapolation of these principles of behavior may well throw light on such topics as homosexuality, mental illness, the abortion controversy, barrenness of couples, divorce, crimes of passion, pornography, pedophilia, and so on. And some understanding of the principles involved might also help in educating young people against such extreme activity.

Please note that the establishment of a controlled pattern of human breeding following eugenics principles as outlined in Chapter 13 might well be able to circumvent almost completely the most undesirable features of the "more natural but violent" human breeding patterns as outlined above. And would that be too large a price to pay for peace, prosperity, and a most rapid and successful approach to a better sustainable world??

On the Role of GOD, the Devil, and Miracles In the World of Modern Science

With the considerable and increasing knowledge of the workings of the world as revealed by the discoveries of modern science, the need for a complete re-evaluation of the authenticity of such postulates as GOD and the Devil in the education of our young folk becomes more and more obvious.

Any scientist with training in the biological sciences knows intuitively that there is no physical basis for the reality of either GOD or the Devil, that GOD did not create the world in seven days, that Eve was not made from Adam's rib, and that Jonah did not live for three days in the belly of a whale. We all know that there was not enough water to flood the whole earth in Noah's day, that Jesus was not born of a virgin, and that in no way did he ever actually change water into wine.

While these stories may have been believable two thousand years ago, we know for certain today that such stories are simply not based on reality. They are simply factually not true. They "do not wash" with what we know of the world today!

And yet such stories persist!! These stories continue to be indoctrinated into the minds of our susceptible youngsters in each succeeding generation with as much determination as if they were absolutely essential ingredients as much required for our proper development as are proteins, vitamins and minerals.

But while such stories are widely recognized today as pure drivel, they seem to be maintained with a vigorous life all of their own. And so we have to ask ourselves, why do we hang on to such stories with so much dogged persistence? There must be a reason for all of that! So what could that reason possibly be?

I believe that we humble humans feel mistakenly that we must maintain that particular teaching framework upon which to hang stories illustrating how we and our youth should hopefully behave, and how we and they hopefully should not behave. These stories are then used in attempts to impress youth with desired moral values. And such old Biblical fables essentially constitute the framework upon which we have traditionally tried to hang those supposedly necessary stories.

But when the framework holding up those traditional old stories is so obviously flawed, the morals that the stories are designated to push tend hopelessly to fall on increasingly deaf ears. And the difficult state in which the youth of our world often finds itself these days may be interpreted as a very strong indication that we had better consider undertaking some major revision of that whole traditional moral-teaching process. Maybe a little more "truth and honesty" on the part of our teaching framework might be the required medicine for today's world.

Let us forget the old story of an imaginary GOD sitting somewhere up there in the sky, with Jesus at his right side. And let us question seriously the claim that they are both there and also at every other place, that they know everything, and that they can accomplish whatever they choose at any time by divine intervention, but usually choose to do nothing at all so that we ordinary humans can adequately express our valuable "freewill".

In reality, it would seem much more accurate to consider that we are all independent units operating here on earth, and that decisions as to what to do or what not to do are made within our own bodies, presumably mostly within our own respective brain systems. And let us admit that, at present, we do not understand as completely as we would like, the exact electrical-biochemical bases on which our human brains operate to make so easily the many decisions that they so successfully are called upon to make on a continuous basis each and every day of our lives.

But we do know that one particular component of our body cells, the chromosomes, does seem to regulate and direct both the building and the operation of those cells that make up that human body. And much has recently been discovered concerning the anatomical nature of those chromosomes, and of their physical structure which is in the form of long chains of nucleic acids

(DNA) tied together in specific information bearing sequences. And those particular sequences determine and effectively regulate the production of enzymes, hormones, structural proteins, and a whole complex raft of other specific biochemical components which together operate to build, maintain, and regulate the operation of the human body. And this includes the operation of the human brain with its capacity to learn, to think, and to predict, as well as to control all necessary operations of the body such as circulation, digestion, temperature control, reproduction, organ repair, and so on and so on.

The human body is thus a most complicated sort of thing, but it would still seem accurate to consider that it all operates according to specific rules of mathematics, upon which the science of physics is built. And upon the science of physics the science of chemistry is built, and upon the science of chemistry the science of biology is built. And upon the science of biology the science of psychology is built. And between the sciences of chemistry and biology, many highly variable, intricate and complex phases of bio-chemistry have developed, and between biology and psychology the field is wide open for huge further development. But the essential point would seem to be that in each and every one of these specific ventures, the working operations follow specific fixed rules that are open to discovery as to how and under which conditions they proceed or do not proceed. And in particular, we do not have to resort to "miracles" or "divine intervention" to explain away any of our achieved experimental results.

Thus it would seem that in the present day and age, it would be both more honest and more productive to erect a new framework upon which to hang stories intended to elucidate our youth on how to live and operate and how not to live and operate. And that future new framework might well be based on the general fields of up to date postulated theory as supported by scientific experimentation. And we might well relegate the Biblical framework of teaching off onto the Department of Ancient History, and not try to push it down the throats of today's youth as a vital and essential part of their present day educational and social development.

As far as the distinction between Right and Wrong is con-

cerned, the choice is as easy to make on the basis of what is beneficial or harmful to the future development of mankind as it is to
choose between the agenda of the Lord or the agenda of the Devil.
Sometimes the distinction is very clear, and sometimes there is a
rather cloudy line between the two. And sometimes one individual
will differ clearly from another individual on a particular specific
point. And this situation parallels the fact that most all of the structural DNA of one individual person is exactly the same as the structural DNA of the second individual, but that in some small specific details, there are always some small significant differences
between every pair of us. And these very small differences can trigger down the line some slight differences in operating conclusions
arrived at by different persons working on exactly the same question. Further to all of that, part of the input going into ultimate decisions, quite a large part actually, comes from a learned or environmental source, and this will always differ in character and amount
from one person to another.

The reasonable means by which to evaluate the Rights or
Wrongs of such specific situations would seem to be an open dia-
logue of a negotiating character undertaken in a democratic type of
environment. And surely, that method would be just as satisfactory,
or better, than the old method of deciding between the agendas of
the Lord and/or the agenda of the Devil. And it would certainly be
a lot more honest and hopefully a lot less argumentative.

Four Building Blocks for a Sustainable Civilization:

A sustainable civilization must be built on four or more basic building blocks. These include (1) Freedom, (2) Wisdom, (3) Power, and (4) Responsibility. Love serves as a strong mortar that tends to hold these building blocks firmly together.

FREEDOM is the foremost of the building blocks of a sustainable civilization. When we are first born, we have no freedom. We are under the complete control of our respective mothers. They in turn are under the heavy control of other persons who essentially/hopefully have been chosen individually by those same respective mothers.

We get our first taste of freedom with our first breath of fresh air, stimulated perhaps by a slap on the buttocks. From that point onward, we have a strong inherited drive to expand our freedom, to the point, in fact, of becoming practically "a little tyrant". We demand everything! And of course, all of the things that we want are not immediately available to us. We thus, through a process of learning, develop a shade of what we might call "wisdom". We choose what to go after, what we can get along without, and how best to go about getting those things that we want most.

If we develop some reasonable level of wisdom quickly, we are given more freedom to pursue those things that we want most. But if we are slow to develop wisdom, our freedom to learn is much more severely restricted. A distinct difference is very soon established between "the haves" and "the have nots". And that distinction is largely established by how fast we learn and employ wisdom, and how fast we learn to employ wisdom depends very much on how much love is bestowed on us in the very beginning. And the amount of love bestowed upon us in the very beginning depends in part on how seriously the child was wanted in the first place. (It also depends in part, of course, upon the wisdom of the mother, the choice of her friends, the environment, and many other such related factors).

It thus becomes most important that each new child be "a wanted child". And if a child will not be very much "a wanted child", it might be better that it would never be born. We may conclude from a consideration of the above that society has very much of a lesson to learn on this particular point.

WISDOM comes in large part from an "opportunity to learn". And our society would do well to provide a very rich environmental opportunity for children to learn. But we should take care to allow as much as possible for them to learn spontaneously, and not to force a lot of fixed, stupid, misguided, religious dogma down their throats. We would be wise here to exercise wisdom to the utmost and to use as much discretion as possible as regards "their opportunity to learn" that we hopefully provide for them with unusual generosity.

POWER. There is a very strong inherited tendency in all of the human race to want to make other people do things "our way" rather than to let them do such things "their own way". We seem to believe strongly that we are certainly smarter/better informed than they are, and so our ways are just naturally better than theirs. Well, maybe they are better at times, but most likely they are not any better, just different. So we end up eventually making related judgments a lot of the time. And usually, we will tend to resist their pressure to leave them to do it their way, and at times that may not be easy for us to do. The result will be that other people will continually be exerting pressure on us "to conform to their wishes", and we might very much NOT WANT to conform to their wishes. And that is where "physical power" comes in, and why it is so necessary to maintain a good reserve of it, and be willing to use it to adequate effect when called upon to do so.

And wisdom is most valuable when it comes to choosing when to use power, and when not to use power. If you will be completely overwhelmed by the power of others in a conflict, it might be better to back down early rather than to be destroyed completely. But there are some points in life over which, I believe, it is most worthwhile to put up a really substantial fight. Wisdom here becomes most important in making that particular choice.

RESPONSIBILITY is taking the credit or blame (mostly seriously the blame) for decisions that you have made by exercising your own brand of wisdom. This becomes most critical when, in the end, your decisions have been proven to have been wrong, or at least not to have been the best decisions possible. And we just MUST be willing to take whatever punishment is metered out ultimately by others for us when we make a firm but bad decision. Otherwise, we become disgraced, and psychologically we become as if dead. In fact, by times we are made forcefully to die physically as punishment for having made such bad choices. Such is life!!

When considering the challenge of fulfilling responsibility, I think of a story told by CBC correspondent Anna Maria Tremonte. During the Bosnian war, she was in Yugoslavia to report on the effects of the war on the ordinary people there. She was housed temporarily with some local families. She found the work highly emotional, and, in effect, very tiring. To the local people, her job of telling their story to the world was of utmost importance.

Those people considered it important that she be well rested to do her job most effectively. So, as she related to us on CBC radio, they offered her the best bed in the place on which to sleep, while many of them slept on the floor. She accepted their generous offer, and subsequently she wrote with compassion to the best of her ability for the information of the outside world the sad story of the plight of those poor suffering peoples.

And that is the story that comes personally first to my mind when I think of the term "fulfilling responsibility".